D0855093

J 332.024 Dak

Dakers, D.
The bottom line.

PRICE:  $17.32 (jn/d  )

DE LA FOSSE BRANCH LIBRARY

# The Bottom Line

## *Money Basics*

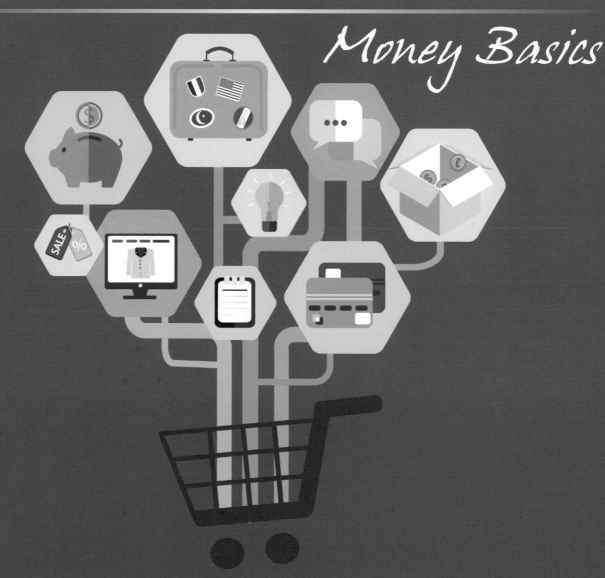

By Diane Dakers

**Educational Consultant:**
Christopher A. Fons
Milwaukee Public Schools

Crabtree Publishing Company
www.crabtreebooks.com

**Financial Literacy for Life**

**Author:** Diane Dakers

**Series research and development:** Reagan Miller

**Project coordinator:** Mark Sachner, Water Buffalo Books

**Editorial director:** Kathy Middleton

**Editors:** Mark Sachner,

**Proofreader:** Wendy Scavuzzo

**Photo research:** Ruth Owen

**Designer:** Westgraphix/Tammy West

**Production coordinator and prepress technician:**
Tammy McGarr

**Print coordinator:** Margaret Amy Salter

**Contributing writer and editor:** Christopher A. Fons,
economics teacher, Riverside University High School,
Milwaukee Public Schools

Written and produced for Crabtree Publishing Company by
Water Buffalo Books

**Photographs:**

Front cover: All images from Shutterstock

Interior:
Alamy: Hoss Mcbain/ZUMA Wire/Alamy Live News: p. 24 (bottom).

Classical Numismatic Group, Inc.: p. 13 (bottom left: both).

Getty Images: Mark Wilson: p. 16.

Public domain: pp. 12 (bottom right), 15 (right).

Shutterstock: pp. 1, 3, 4, 5, 6, 7 (top), 8, 9, 10, 11, 13 (top), 15 (left),
17, 18, 19, 20, 22 (top and bottom), 23, 24 (top: both), 25, 26, 27,
29 (bottom right), 30, 31, 33 (bottom), 36, 37 (left and center),
40, 42, 43; Ababil Wings SS: p. 22 (middle); AzriSuratmin: p. 29
(bottom left); charnsitr: p. 33 (middle); Kenary820: p. 29 (top);
Toni Genes: p. 33 (top); Victor Maschek: p. 38.

Water Buffalo Books: pp. 28, 34, 37 (right).

Wikipedia Creative Commons: pp. 7 (bottom), 12 (top and bottom
left), 13 (bottom right: all), 14.

**Library and Archives Canada Cataloguing in Publication**

Dakers, Diane, author
     The bottom line : money basics / Diane Dakers.

(Financial literacy for life)
Includes index.
Issued in print and electronic formats.
ISBN 978-0-7787-3095-8 (hardcover).--
ISBN 978-0-7787-3104-7 (softcover).--
ISBN 978-1-4271-1874-5 (HTML)

     1. Finance, Personal--Juvenile literature. 2. Financial literacy--Juvenile
literature. I. Title.

HG179.D342 2017         j332.024        C2016-907137-5
                                               C2016-907138-3

**Library of Congress Cataloging-in-Publication Data**

CIP available at the Library of Congress

## Crabtree Publishing Company

www.crabtreebooks.com     1-800-387-7650

Printed in Canada/062017/MA20170420

Copyright © **2017 CRABTREE PUBLISHING COMPANY.** All rights reserved. No part of this publication may be reproduced, stored in a retrieval system
or be transmitted in any form or by any means, electronic, mechanical, photocopying, recording, or otherwise, without the prior written permission of Crabtree
Publishing Company. In Canada: We acknowledge the financial support of the Government of Canada through the Canada Book Fund for our publishing activities.

**Published in Canada**
**Crabtree Publishing**
616 Welland Ave.
St. Catharines, Ontario
L2M 5V6

**Published in the United States**
**Crabtree Publishing**
PMB 59051
350 Fifth Avenue, 59th Floor
New York, New York 10118

**Published in the United Kingdom**
**Crabtree Publishing**
Maritime House
Basin Road North, Hove
BN41 1WR

**Published in Australia**
**Crabtree Publishing**
3 Charles Street
Coburg North
VIC 3058

# Contents

# MONEY MAKES THE WORLD GO 'ROUND

Moolah. Bread. Bucks. Dough. Dinero. Loot. Cabbage. Coinage. Scratch. Smackers. Whatever you call it, you can't live without it. Everyone needs money. It pays for the necessities in life—food, clothing, shelter, health care, and transportation. Many of us will struggle to have enough money for those necessities. And even if we have enough to live on, most of us wish we had more of it. That's because money also allows us to have fun. We use money to take an occasional vacation or to buy the latest gadgets.

A laptop and a credit card will help you get what you want in life. But before you hit "submit" for those online purchases, you should think about the bigger picture of bills and other **expenses** that need to be paid every month!

# For Richer or Poorer...

Some people believe "money is power." To others, it's "the root of all evil." Whether you're struggling to make enough to get by, or spending it like water, it's important to understand how money works, learn to manage it well, and develop a healthy relationship with it. After all, it's going to be in your life for a long, long time.

## Money Matters

Some people have a love-hate relationship with money. They love that it can buy them the things they want to live a certain lifestyle. On the other hand, people hate money when they don't have enough to meet their needs, fulfill their dreams, or do everything they want to do in life. Lack of money can be one of the greatest sources of frustration in a person's lifetime—but it doesn't always have to be.

Money, especially shared money, is also the subject of arguments. Married couples, for example, often have different ideas about how they should spend their hard-earned money. One of them might want to **splurge** on a tropical vacation, while the other wants to buy a new house. They may not realize that, with proper planning, they can probably do both.

Money stirs up other emotions in people, too—worry that they don't have enough to pay the bills, guilt over spending instead of saving, or jealousy toward wealthy people who seem to have more than their fair share.

If the answer to the question "What's in your wallet?" is "Not nearly enough," then you may need to sit down and balance some factors, such as these: what you need, what you want, how much money you earn, and what you can afford to spend and save. It's all a part of becoming financially **savvy**!

# Financial Literacy

**$PEAKING OF MONEY...**
"I'm passionate about financial literacy. I want to live in a financially literate society. I want kids to understand the importance of savings and **investing**. [...] It's crucial that people understand the importance of financial literacy, because it's actually life saving."

Mellody Hobson,
American businesswoman

## Sharpen Your Financial Smarts

Rather than going through life worrying, feeling guilty, and experiencing jealousy, you can choose to have a healthier relationship with your dollars and cents. You can choose to sharpen your money smarts. This area of expertise is called financial literacy, and it's something you can start working on right now.

## Learn the Language of Money

Financial literacy is about learning the language of money and becoming comfortable speaking that language. It's about understanding how to earn money, keep track of it, and save and spend it wisely. Mostly, financial literacy is about learning how money works, and how it can work for you.

Many people consider money to be a **taboo** subject, or something that is not acceptable to talk about in public. Not talking about money, though, is one of the things that can lead to financial problems in life.

### WORK

### KEEP TRACK

### SPEND & SAVE

### SUCCEED

Earning money, keeping track of it, and spending and saving wisely are some of the important ingredients leading to financial literacy and success.

We all need money for even the simplest, least expensive necessities of life. Having *lots* of money can buy incredibly expensive things, such as the Koenigsegg CCXR Trevita Supercar shown below. It's yours for $4.8 million! But can even a fraction of that money buy you the love of an animal or a shared moment with your friends?

## BE CAREFUL OUT THERE

# IT CAN'T BUY HAPPINESS

It's tempting to think that having lots of money would solve all of life's problems. If you could buy anything you wanted, travel to any country in the world, and live in a mansion with servants and a swimming pool, you'd be totally happy, right?

Not necessarily.

It's important to have enough money to buy the things we need to survive, and it certainly helps to have enough money to live a comfortable life, but that's not the only thing you need to be happy. Think of all the things that make you smile—your best friends, your dog, playing your favorite sports, or beating your big sister in a race to the park. You can probably think of dozens more things you enjoy that don't cost money!

Being happy is a blend of many different ingredients. One of those ingredients is having enough money to feel financially **secure**.

# Putting Money in Its Place

Many people barely think about money. They earn it and spend it. Some of these people might run out of money, and wonder where it has gone. They lack financial security. That means they don't have the peace of mind that comes with knowing they have enough money—for today's expenses and for tomorrow's dreams (or emergencies).

Becoming financially secure requires that you think about your money, make plans for it, and keep track of it. It means taking charge of your dollars and cents. It means understanding what money can (and cannot) do for you, where it comes from, and where it goes.

Doing all this thinking upfront means you won't have to stress about money later. That's because you are setting yourself up to be financially secure, with a solid plan in place.

It's important to develop a healthy, lifelong relationship with money, so you can meet your goals without financial fears running your life.

The first step in creating a positive partnership with money is to be clear about what it is. Why do we have money? Who invented it? Where does it come from? How does it work? The answers to some of these questions are ancient history.

A good place to start on the path to financial security is to think about where money does—and does not—come from!

# SHOW ME THE MONEY!

Believe it or not, that ten-dollar bill burning a hole in your pocket has no *actual* value. It's simply a fancy piece of paper. In our society, though, we have all agreed that this particular fancy piece of paper can be exchanged for ten dollars' worth of stuff. Whether it's bills or coins (or beads or seashells), that's what money is—something that can be exchanged for something else. It has no *real* value, but it *represents* value, and we all agree to accept it as a form of payment. Today's ten-dollar bill is pretty easy to carry around. But **currency** hasn't always been this convenient.

## Before Currency Was Current

Money may not grow on trees, but thousands of years ago, it could be found in fields. Of course, it wasn't like today's currency. Back then, humans got things by trading with each other.

Some of the first things people used to trade, or **barter**, were cows, sheep, and camels. Then came wheat, vegetables, and other plants.

Until about 3,000 years ago, bartering was the main way humans exchanged goods and services. For example, a cow might be traded for some corn or tomatoes, or a sheep's fleece bartered for a bundle of wheat.

Bartering is still sometimes used today. Services such as plumbing and carpentry work might be traded for one another. Often goods, such as bakery products and knitted clothing, might be exchanged for one another. But historically, swapping goods has often come with a few problems.

## So how many tomatoes d'ya want for that cow?

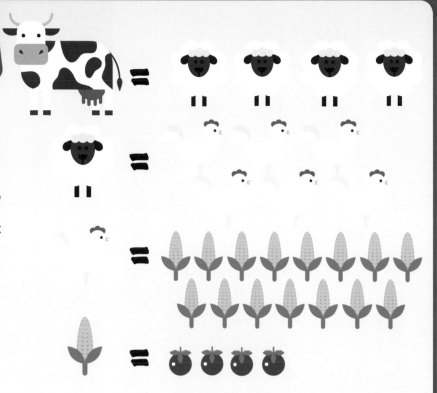

Bartering, or trading, can take skill, luck, and a bit of nerve! Who chooses how many sheep a cow is worth? Or how many chickens it takes to get one sheep? And if two people agree on that, how many chickens—or other goods—might it take to get that cow?

Get a pencil, calculator, and piece of paper. See if you can figure out, based on the goods shown here, how many tomatoes a cow is worth. Does this "price" seem fair to you? (The answer is at the bottom of the page.)

## Time and Money

First of all, an ear of corn, a bunch of tomatoes, and a cow have different values. Who decides how many tomatoes a cow is worth? Bartering requires that two people agree that their items have equal value.

Secondly, sheep might be **shorn** in early spring, but wheat isn't ready for harvest until late summer or fall. If farmers

needed sheep's wool in the spring, they wouldn't have any wheat ready to barter. The timing of the exchange has to make sense, but schedules don't always match. Therefore, taking something in the spring with a promise of "payment" in the fall might not be convenient for both traders.

In "Jack and the Beanstalk," everything turned out pretty well for Jack when he traded the family cow for a handful of beans. Bartering in the real world, however, rarely works like a fairy tale!

1 cow = 1,440 tomatoes!

## Keeping It Fresh

Another problem with bartering goods might be storage. Imagine a farmer wants to exchange eggs for a donkey. The farmer probably wouldn't be able to store eggs and keep them fresh long enough to collect a donkey's worth of omelets. On the other hand, you can't cut a donkey in half to pay for a week's worth of eggs. It's not always possible to exchange goods and services in a way that is equal.

## Coming Up with a Better Idea

For reasons like these, by about 1200 BCE, it became clear that humans needed a better system. They needed something with an agreed-upon value that could be exchanged for goods and services—something small, standard-sized, and practical.

The first currency that fit the bill in those days was a type of seashell. For the next 500 years, the **cowrie** shell, found in the Indian and

Cowrie shells were once a common form of currency in many parts of the world.

Pacific oceans, was used around the world. Some African countries still accepted cowries as currency into the mid-20th century.

The first metal coins—simple metal discs—came into being in China around 650 BCE. Because they had no actual value, though, it was difficult to trade them for goods. The kingdom of Lydia, in what is now Turkey, was the first government to "**mint**," or issue, coins. Made of precious metals, such as gold or silver, these coins were stamped with official images and words. They weren't always the same size and shape, and their value was determined by weighing them—they were, literally, worth their weight in gold.

This print from the mid-1800s shows an Arab merchant trading goods for cowrie shells.

Many of the first metal coins in China were miniature versions of familiar tools. This bronze coin, dating from sometime around 500 BCE., was made to resemble a spade, or shovel, and is known as a "spade coin."

## THINK FOR YOURSELF

### Bartering Today

People have been bartering, or trading goods for other goods, for thousands of years. Today, we usually measure the worth of an object by its financial, or dollar, value. But often, instead of using money, people trade things. Sometimes they trade things casually, among family and friends, sometimes by posting a notice in a newspaper or on a bulletin board, and sometimes by searching on the internet for things that others would like to trade.

Have you ever bartered anything with your friends or family? Think about the things people you know have swapped. Have they traded only objects, or other things, such as favors or services? Who do you think did better in these swaps? If you were doing the bartering, how might you have handled the deal?

## "Fixing" the Value of Money

Before long, the Lydians began **standardizing** the coins, so they didn't have to weigh them every time they used them. The concept of standardized, or fixed-value, coins soon spread throughout Greece, the Middle East, and the Roman Empire. However, carrying around enough coins to make large purchases, such as a farm, could be a weighty exercise. To solve this problem, the Chinese began making money out of leather, linen, bamboo, and paper around the year 800.

Both sides of a Lydian coin, made from a mixture of gold and silver, dating back to around 500 BCE.

An assortment of ancient Roman coins, some dating back to 250 BCE.

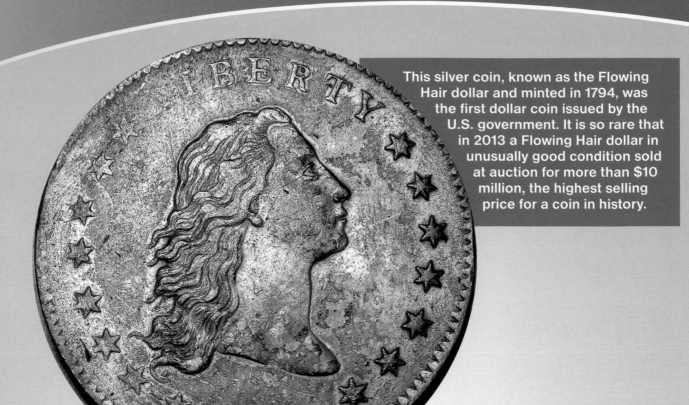

This silver coin, known as the Flowing Hair dollar and minted in 1794, was the first dollar coin issued by the U.S. government. It is so rare that in 2013 a Flowing Hair dollar in unusually good condition sold at auction for more than $10 million, the highest selling price for a coin in history.

Still, it wasn't exactly like today's money—it was a practice called a **transferable receipt system**. Back then, an individual would lug his or her gold and silver to an ancient bank and hand it over. In exchange, the banker issued a **receipt** for the precious metals. The person could then trade the receipt for goods at a shop. The merchant who sold the goods, in turn, transferred the same receipt to another merchant to purchase something else. And so on.

At any time, whoever had the receipt could exchange it for the original stash of gold and silver at the bank. But why do that when it was easier to carry a piece of paper in your pocket?

## Paper Currency Goes International

European banks adopted this system of paper receipts in the 1500s. A century later, European governments (rather than banks) began issuing paper currencies with standardized values.

Around the same time, Massachusetts became the first **colony** in America to **circulate** its own money. For the next two centuries, different colonial currencies came and went in North America. Finally, in 1792, the United States adopted the dollar as its official currency and established the U.S. Mint to make coins. In 1862, the government of the United States began printing paper money.

# Making Money by Faking Money?
# Think Again!

It would be nice if, when your wallet is empty, you could simply photocopy a few bills and continue shopping. But it doesn't work that way, and it's not that simple.

Making new money can take years of design, technology, and security work before it is approved as currency.

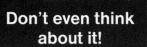

**Don't even think about it!**

In most countries, a single organization is assigned to print **banknotes**, or bills. In the United States, for example, the Bureau of Engraving and Printing is the only organization allowed to make new paper money. In Canada, it's the Bank of Canada. Coins in those countries are made by the U.S. Mint and the Royal Canadian Mint, respectively.

For all moneymakers, security is the number-one **priority**. Today, people who create **counterfeit** money have access to the same cutting-edge technology as official printers do, and these criminals work hard to create bogus bills. To make paper money hard to fake, currency designers add all kinds of security features—some obvious, some secret—to foil the fraudsters.

**THINK FOR YOURSELF**

Zoom in on a detail of a U.S. ten-dollar bill, featuring a portrait of Alexander Hamilton, the first U.S. Secretary of the Treasury (and the subject of the runaway hit musical *Hamilton*!). If you look closely, you can see several tiny number "10" symbols below the serial number and to the left of Hamilton. The zeros of these 10s form a pattern that can be detected by special anti-counterfeiting programs in color photocopying machines. Once these patterns are detected, the machines will not reproduce the bills.

## What's Up with *That*?

Have you ever noticed people accepting your money at a store or restaurant doing anything unusual with the bills you hand them? Do they pick up the currency and hold it to the light at an angle? What do you think they're looking for? And what about when they take a marker and draw a line on a bill? What could that be about? Look at the bills you have in your wallet, or the ones you get back as change. Do you see any clues about why your money gets such special treatment?

Of course, if you know someone who works behind a cash register, you could also ask them. See how much they know about what goes on with the money that passes through their hands!

## The U.S. Greenback...

In the United States, the paper used for money is made from a mix of cotton and linen. The paper goes through three separate printing processes to turn it into legal currency. The first step is to run giant sheets of this paper through a machine that prints images on both sides at the same time. The second process adds **tactile** elements to the bills. These are raised features you can feel with your fingers. Finally, the giant sheets of paper are cut up and trimmed to dollar-bill-sized pieces and stamped with serial numbers and official seals. The U.S. Bureau of Engraving and Printing produces 38 million of these banknotes every day!

Until 2003, all U.S. banknotes were green—thus the name "greenback." Beginning that year, printers included subtle splashes of color in the bills, as an added security feature.

A worker inspects sheets of newly printed one-dollar bills at the Bureau of Engraving and Printing in Washington, D.C. Once these bills have been trimmed to size, they will be individually stamped with official seals and serial numbers, so each bill will have a unique identity.

## FOCUS ON FINANCE

## Plastic Fantastic: From Paper to Polymer

In 1988, Australia became the first country to do away with paper money and replace it with plastic, or **polymer**, bank notes. Today, eight nations around the world use polymer bills, with a number of others in the process of making the paper-to-plastic switch.

Between 2011 and 2013, Canada replaced paper money with polymer notes. The smooth, shiny bills are harder to counterfeit, they last longer, and they are more environmentally friendly. When they wear out, they are shredded and recycled into other plastic products.

Polymer money also allows for extra security features, such as metallic images, **holographic** stripes, and clear and frosted windows that contain hidden pictures and text. The redesign is doing its job. Since the new bills came into circulation, counterfeiting in Canada has dropped by 90 percent.

## ...and Canuck Bucks

Many residents of the United States who visit Canada for the first time are surprised at the look of Canadian money. "It looks like Monopoly money," some say. That's because Canadian money is colorful, shiny, and see-through in places. Plus, it's made of plastic. It's also one of the world's hardest-to-copy currencies.

Ever since the Bank of Canada began printing money in 1935, Canadian money has been brightly colored. Today, the five-dollar bill is blue, the ten is purple, and the fifty is red. The only greenback in Canada is the twenty-dollar bill.

## Easy Money: ATMs and Debit Cards

It wasn't that long ago when the only way to get money to pay for things was to go to the bank. To complicate money matters further, banks kept shorter hours than other businesses. Most **financial institutions** opened at 10:00 in the morning and closed at 3:00 or 4:00 in the afternoon. They were also closed on weekends.

# F O CUS
## ON FINANCE

### Creating Coins

Coins are made out of chunks of metal, usually blends of copper, steel, tin, nickel, or zinc. The metal is cut into blank coin shapes, which are then washed and polished. Using great pressure, a machine stamps images into both sides of the blanks at the same time. And ta-da, the metal is now money!

In the late 1960s, a number of individual banks around the world—in the UK (London) and United States (New York City), as well as in Sweden and Japan—changed financial history when they launched the first-ever 24-hour cash machines. The original machines had **glitches** and took a long time to catch on. But by the mid-1980s, most banking networks around the world had adopted the devices, now called Automated (or Automatic) Teller Machines, or **ATMs**. Today, they are everywhere—even in Antarctica.

This 50-dollar bill shows the variety of coloring and other features that have helped Canadian currency, which is now made of polymer, relatively difficult to counterfeit.

Swipe, scan, or insert your card. Enter the correct PIN (personal identification number) for your account. Take your cash. ATMs provide bank and credit-card customers with quick access to their accounts.

With the increase of ATMs through the 1980s, **debit cards** became popular. At first, debit cards only worked at cash machines. By the early 1990s, however, many stores and businesses accepted them as a method of **point-of-sale** payment, in addition to cash, checks, and credit cards.

## Going High-Tech: The Evolution or Extinction of Money?

Since then, digital technology has allowed money to further evolve. Today, we can **withdraw** money from an ATM, pay for a store purchase with a debit or credit card, transfer money by email, update our bank accounts electronically, and even pay by scanning our smartphones.

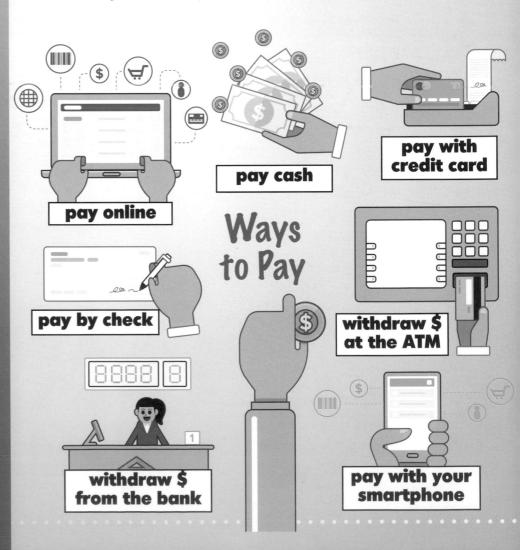

pay online

pay cash

pay with credit card

pay by check

Ways to Pay

withdraw $ at the ATM

withdraw $ from the bank

pay with your smartphone

In 2014, only 14 percent of all purchases in the United States were made with cash. The use of credit cards and other electronic means of payment is much higher. Some people predict that it won't be long before we are a completely cashless society.

Still, whether your money is real or **virtual**, it's important that you know how to manage it.

Today, debit and credit cards have computer chips that can be read to access our bank and credit accounts. We also implant scannable microchips in cats and dogs to help ID and find our lost pets. Many feel that the day isn't far off when similar microchips may be implanted beneath our skin that we can use to instantly pay for things! Will we be financially smart enough to manage money when it's no longer something we can touch or see?

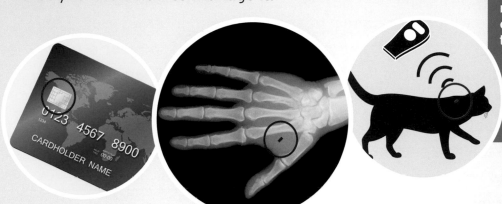

# BE CAREFUL OUT THERE

# THE GOVERNMENT CAN'T JUST MAKE MORE!

If many citizens needed extra money, you might think the government could just make more. Unfortunately, printing, or minting, extra money leads to more problems than it solves.

Say the government simply started handing out cash to whoever needed it. Suddenly, there would be a lot of money out there, and people could start buying more stuff. That means stores might run out of goods to sell. To make sure they keep their stores stocked, merchants raise prices so fewer people buy the goods. That, in turn, means **consumers** need more money to pay for the same things. This is called **inflation**.

Governments work hard to control inflation. If they don't, either prices skyrocket and nobody can afford to buy anything, or money becomes meaningless and you'd need a wheelbarrow-full to buy the smallest thing.

# CHAPTER THREE

# COMMON CENT$

Right now, the adults in your life probably take care of the finances for your family. They buy groceries, furniture for your home, and gas for the car. They pay the rent or **mortgage**, heating bills, and internet fees. They probably take care of most of your personal expenses, too—your school supplies, clothing, and music lessons. Juggling all these financial factors, while trying to save money for the future, is a complicated business. You may think you're too young to have to think about any of it. In fact, though, you are at the *perfect* age to start learning how to organize all the money that will be coming and going throughout your life.

You're never too young to have an idea of how many places your money can go. Here are just a few expenses that will take a chunk out of your monthly earnings as you get older. Are any of them things you are already paying for?

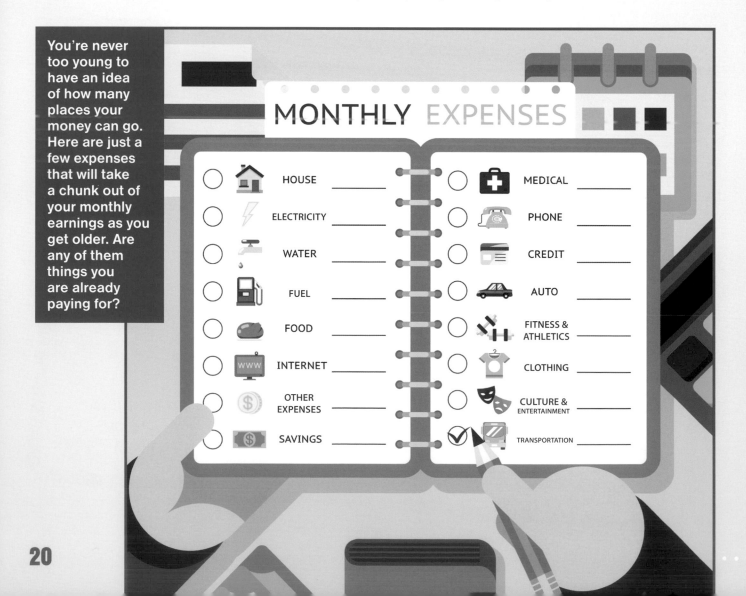

MONTHLY EXPENSES

○ HOUSE _____
○ ELECTRICITY _____
○ WATER _____
○ FUEL _____
○ FOOD _____
○ INTERNET _____
○ OTHER EXPENSES _____
○ SAVINGS _____

○ MEDICAL _____
○ PHONE _____
○ CREDIT _____
○ AUTO _____
○ FITNESS & ATHLETICS _____
○ CLOTHING _____
○ CULTURE & ENTERTAINMENT _____
✓ TRANSPORTATION _____

## Smart Money

If you're like most people, when you get your hands on some cash, you spend it. It's fun to go out with your friends, buy a new video game, or spoil yourself with a new pair of shoes! There's nothing wrong with that, now and then.

But what if you want to buy something big, such as a new bicycle? If money slips through your fingers quickly, that bike may never be anything but a faraway dream. Sometimes, too, spending all your money right away means there's nothing left for unexpected emergencies.

Many people spend their hard-earned money without thinking. They make no plans for it. Often, the only time people think about where their money goes is when it's already gone.

## The Paycheck-to-Paycheck Cycle

More than half of American adults live "**paycheck-to-paycheck**." That means they receive a paycheck at work, spend their money, and have nothing left until the next payday. They never get ahead. They can never save for something special. They never set aside a stash of cash for emergencies. It's a frustrating way to live.

The best way to keep yourself from falling into this cycle is to start managing your money now. That might sound boring, but it's not. It can be fun to watch your money grow! If you pay attention to your spending, plan your purchases, and set saving targets, you'll be surprised at how quickly you can meet your financial goals–and maybe even buy that bicycle.

## Thinking Ahead

"Money management" probably sounds deadly dull to you. You might think "financial planning" means putting all your money in the bank. It might make you fear that you'll never have cash for fun things such as going to the movies, or buying clothes or a new smartphone. But that's not what it's all about.

Financial planning simply means giving some thought to the things you want and need, and coming up with a plan to get them. It means balancing spending money with saving money. It means knowing where your money comes from and where it goes.

It also means setting goals. These might include buying that new bicycle, pulling together a stash of spending money for a family vacation, or treating yourself to a new laptop. By setting financial goals, and thinking about how you spend your dollars, you'll eventually be able to afford those big-ticket items.

**Short-Term Goal**

**Medium-Term Goal**

**Long-Term Goal**

## Make a Want List

The first step in reaching your financial goals is to figure out what they are. Start dreaming. Make a want list!

The items on your want or wish list will probably fall into three categories:

1. **Things you can afford now with the money you have.**
2. **Small things that a few weeks' allowance will cover.**
3. **Large things (like that bike) that you'll have to save for.**

These are called **short-term**, **medium-term**, and **long-term** financial goals. A **short-term goal** might be to buy a comic book or magazine, a fast-food lunch with friends, or a bottle of nail polish. A **medium-term goal** might be to get a complex Lego set, a skateboard, an inexpensive smart watch, or a birthday gift for a friend. **Long-term goals** could include buying that bike, a tablet, or a TV for your bedroom.

As you grow older, the things that make up your goals will shift or change entirely. For example, your short-term goals will probably still include food and entertainment with friends. But your medium- and long-term goals may now include saving for a car, paying monthly rent, buying a home, or, once you get a regular job, saving for when you retire.

These are serious goals, and they are important to keep in mind even when, as a kid, your goals are less complex!

Here are some things (shown at right) that you might skip or cut back on to save for a long-term financial goal. Let's say you have your eye on a tablet that sells for $300. Do you think you can stick with this plan until you've saved enough to break open that piggy bank and make your big purchase?

**Skip lunch with friends once a week.**

SAVE $4

**Drink water instead of soda five times a week.**

SAVE $5

SAVE $10

**Walk instead of taking the bus five times a week.**

SAVE $3

**Skip a snack on the way home twice a week**

## Sorting Out Your Priorities

Now that you have created your want list, take a look at it. Which items are the most important to you? If buying a TV is more important to you than having lunch out with your friends every day, make a note of that. It doesn't mean you'll never again have lunch out with your friends. It simply means you're starting to think about what matters to you. Maybe, by skipping the occasional lunch out with friends, you can bank a bit of extra money to get you closer to buying that tablet.

The idea is to figure out which things matter to you most, and what choices you're willing to make to get them.

Remember, if you spend all your money as soon as you get it, you may never reach your medium- or long-term financial goals. Sure, it can be more fun to blow your bucks on music, movies, or munchies than to bank them.

## MAKE A WANT LIST CHART

**Give It a Try, and DIY**

Studies show that writing down your goals makes them more likely to become reality. So start writing! Make a chart with 5 columns. You will fill out two now, and three later on, when we get to Chapter 4. See page 35 for a sample of this chart.

1. In column #1, the left-hand column of your chart, list all the things you want that cost money. These may include things you want to buy and things you want to do.

2. In column #2, note whether each item is a short-, medium-, or long-term goal.

3. Use star stickers or highlighters in different colors, to label each item as low, medium, or high priority.

But if you save a portion of your weekly allowance, or a bit of your birthday money, you'll be surprised at how quickly those dollars will add up to the purchase price of a tablet, concert tickets, or a blingy necklace.

**DESIGNER JEANS: $150**

**CHEAP JEANS: $35**

## What Do You Really, Really Want?

Now that you've thought about everything you *want*, it's time to consider the things you *need*. Chances are that your wants and needs are not the same.

For example, you might *need* a new pair of jeans, but what you *want* is the latest designer fashion. This is where you start making choices. In this case, if being stylish is important to you, you could choose to spend big bucks

If you compare the difference in price between a pair of designer jeans and a cheaper pair, you'll be able to see how your priorities stack up. Taking your time and thinking things through before buying doesn't sound like much fun. But you'll feel better when you figure out how using your financial smarts can help you save for something big down the road!

**TAYLOR SWIFT CONCERT with 80,000 of her closest friends: $180**

### BE CAREFUL OUT THERE
# KEEP IT REAL!

When setting financial goals, make sure they are realistic. Buying a model airplane kit next month is probably realistic. Buying a *real* airplane next month or next year is probably not. However, it might be realistic for you to buy a real airplane in 15 years. If that's something you want to do, put it on your want list—in the long-long-long-term goal category!

on the designer duds. If, on the other hand, it's more important to you to go to a Taylor Swift concert a few months down the road, you could choose to buy less expensive jeans and save some money toward a ticket to the show.

Many consumers—adults and kids alike—spend their money without thinking. All they know is, "I want this, and I want it now." So they buy it, whatever it may be. This is called an **impulse buy**, and it's usually an in-the-moment want, not a need.

Impulse buying is spending money without planning. It often results in paying more than you should have paid for an item, or acquiring things you don't want or need. Often, people suffer **"buyer's remorse"** after an impulse buy. This means they regret spending their money on something they later realize they didn't need.

## A Pop Quiz to Test Your Needs

If you're not sure if something is a need or a want, try living without it for a while. If you can survive without it, it's probably a want, not a need.

impulse buy now...

SALE SALE SALE

...buyer's remorse later

## Be on the Alert for Impulse Buys

There's nothing wrong with the occasional inexpensive impulse buy—a candy bar at the supermarket checkout, or a last-minute lip balm. It can become tricky, though, if that's the only kind of buying you do. It's a sure-fire way to run out of moolah before you even realize it's gone.

Some people impulse buy because they're in a good mood, and buying new items helps them stay in a good mood. Other people buy stuff to cheer themselves up when they're feeling down.

Peer pressure is another reason individuals spend money on things they don't need. If everyone in your class has an MP3 player, for example, you might feel that you need one, too. And if you've ever browsed online, you know how hard it can be to resist loading up your virtual shopping cart. It's especially hard when things you order online can be delivered in a day...or even a few hours!

*Where* you spend your time can also influence your spending. Some people can't go to a movie without buying an expensive bag of popcorn and a soda.

For people truly interested in saving money, and reaching financial goals, these are the kinds of spending situations to pay attention to. Focusing on saving money doesn't mean you'll *never* buy popcorn at a movie, but maybe, from now on, you'll choose to buy a smaller bag, or you won't buy popcorn *every* time you go to the movies. Over time, these small savings will add up, and help you achieve your medium- and long-term financial goals. It's all about thinking before you spend.

With some thought and planning ahead, you can figure out how to get that bike you've been dreaming of and have fun at the movies!

## MAKE A NEED LIST CHART

Now that you've made your want list, make a second chart for your needs. Again, make a five-column chart—you'll fill in the final three columns later. See page 35 for a sample of this chart.

1. This time, in column #1 write down all the things you need money for. That might include personal toiletries, a new collar for your dog, or a birthday present for your annoying little brother.

2. In column #2, make note of when you have to buy, or pay for, each item. Identify short-, medium-, and long-term needs.

3. Compare your want list and your need list. Are any items on both lists?

## THINK FOR YOURSELF

### Get Your Priorities Straight!

Look at your want list and your need list. Arrange the items in a diagram, like the one shown. Called a Venn diagram, it compares the similarities and differences of two topics. This Venn diagram groups things kids might want (yellow) and need (blue). In some cases, things kids want might also be things they need (green). What kinds of financial decisions might you make about items that are in the "green zone" of a diagram like this one?

**WANT LIST**

**NEED LIST**

snacks with friends

smart TV

skateboard

magazine subscription

food

bicycle

jeans

laptop

daily lunch

new clothes

internet access

transportation

27

## Manage Your Impulses!

One way to avoid impulse buys is to learn to separate your *needs* from your *wants*. It's also a good idea to take time to look for sales, to think about how much you can afford to spend on an item, and to compare prices at different stores and online.

Another trick is to make two shopping trips, and more than one visit online, before you spend money. In other words, you can make a looking trip, and a buying trip. If you leave your money at home when you're "just looking," you won't be tempted to spend without thinking—and nobody will be able to talk you into paying for something you don't really need or want.

When you finally make the perfect purchase at the perfect price, you'll feel like a super shopper: a smart consumer, with no buyer's remorse. You'll also have a little more money to help meet your longer-term goals!

Now that you know what those goals are—and you've thought about which ones are most important to you—it's time to take the next steps in your financial planning process. It's time to get organized, so you can make those dreams come true!

## BE CAREFUL OUT THERE

### LOOK BEFORE YOU LEAP... EVEN IF IT'S ONLY A BUCK!

Retailers know that customers tend to buy on impulse. That's why they place lots of small, inexpensive items at the cash register. They know a customer who's waiting to pay for their items is easily tempted to add a candy bar, a colorful magazine, or a key chain to their cart while they're in line. As a buyer, you might think, "Oh, it's only a dollar. I can afford that." However, these small purchases can add up to a lot of wasted money. Think before you're tempted! What might be a better use of that dollar?

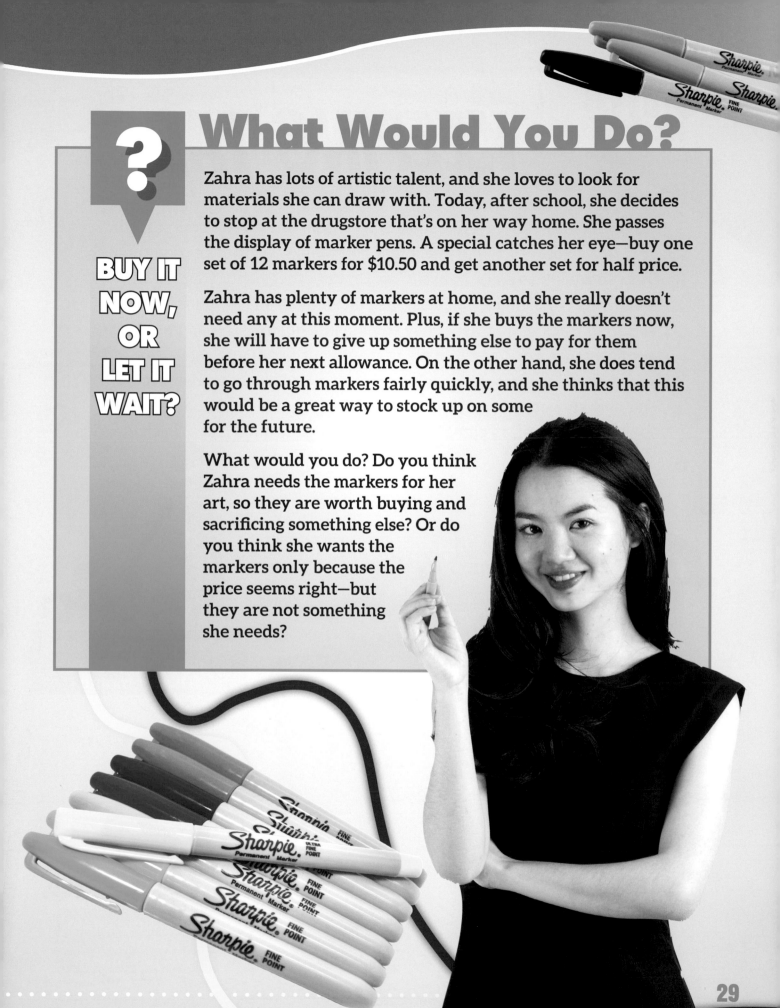

# What Would You Do?

## BUY IT NOW, OR LET IT WAIT?

Zahra has lots of artistic talent, and she loves to look for materials she can draw with. Today, after school, she decides to stop at the drugstore that's on her way home. She passes the display of marker pens. A special catches her eye—buy one set of 12 markers for $10.50 and get another set for half price.

Zahra has plenty of markers at home, and she really doesn't need any at this moment. Plus, if she buys the markers now, she will have to give up something else to pay for them before her next allowance. On the other hand, she does tend to go through markers fairly quickly, and she thinks that this would be a great way to stock up on some for the future.

What would you do? Do you think Zahra needs the markers for her art, so they are worth buying and sacrificing something else? Or do you think she wants the markers only because the price seems right—but they are not something she needs?

# KEEPING TABS

Money usually comes into people's lives from one or two sources. For you, those sources of **income** might be a weekly allowance or earnings from shoveling snow or babysitting. On the other hand, your list of wants and needs (your financial goals) may include dozens of items. How do you keep track of all this money coming and going? How do you figure out how much you need to save to meet your financial goals? How much spending money should you give yourself every week, or every month? You probably get a headache just thinking about it all. But managing your money is not as complicated as you might think.

**shoveling snow (winter): around $10 per snowfall**

Where does my monthly income come from?

**mowing grandparents' lawn (summer): $10 per month**

**babysitting for my cousin: $5 per hour**

**doing household chores: $20 per month**

> **Hey! Budgeting is a little like straightening up my room. The more I do it, the easier it gets!**

## The Game Plan

One of the main tools used to organize money is a **budget**. This is a document that tracks where your money comes from (income), and where you're going to spend it (expenses). Many people fear budgeting because they think it takes too much time, that it won't work for them, or that it will take the fun out of spending money.

Because fewer than half of all American adults follow budgets, many kids never learn how to make one. The reality is that creating—and sticking to—a budget will help you reach your financial goals faster than you would without it. Budgeting is all about making choices about where, and how, you want to dole out your dollars.

It requires some thought to make a budget, and self-control to stick to it. At first, it might feel overwhelming to track every dollar that comes and goes. Before long, though, it becomes habit. You'll be tracking your spending and savings without even thinking about it.

## The Joys of Budgeting

Some people believe budgets make life boring. That's not true. In fact, budgets can actually make life more fun.

Think of your finances as your room, and think of budgeting as the financial version of cleaning your room. If your room is organized, you can find all your things without getting frustrated and upset. If your room is always a mess, however, straightening it out becomes more difficult with each passing day.

The longer it takes you to straighten up your room, the harder it will be to find things, and the more frustrating, and less fun, it is to be there.

It's the same with money. You may be *used* to living without a budget, but that doesn't make life *easier*. It just makes it harder to get organized.

Like a cleaned-up room, your budget makes it easier to have what you need *and* what you want. That's why you can make room for "**mad money**" in your budget to spend on fun stuff. Then you'll have enough to spend on yourself and on things that are important.

## Cut Yourself Some Slack!

You still might overspend now and again. Don't be hard on yourself if that happens—just pay attention to what you bought, why you bought it, and how much you spent. If it happens over and over again, you might need to adjust your budget.

Budgeting is about making your life easier. The goals of making, and following, a budget are to develop good habits, clarify financial goals, and find ways to make your money work for you.

## Money for Today—and for Tomorrow

The first step in creating a budget is to be clear about where your money comes from and where it goes.

Where do you get your spending money? Your income sources might include a weekly allowance, birthday money or gift cards, a scholarship from school, or money you earn from walking the neighbor's dog, delivering newspapers, or doing odd jobs in the community.

Now think about the other side of the equation—where do you spend your money? This question isn't so easy to answer. You might *think* you know where your money goes, but if you're like many people, you spend money without even realizing it.

Once you get a sense of where your money comes from, and where you're spending it, you can begin to make informed, or thoughtful, choices. This is where your financial goals come in.

## BE CAREFUL OUT THERE

## MAKE YOUR BUDGET WORK FOR YOU

When you first make a budget and start following it, you might find that it is too strict for you, and you need to change it. On the other hand, it's possible that you'll discover you have money left over at the end of each week or month. Either way, it's important to make adjustments to your budget so that you can find the right balance between spending and saving. A budget is a document that's meant to be reviewed, updated, and fine-tuned as needed. It has to fit you, your lifestyle, and your goals.

## A Good Place to Start

A good way to start organizing, or budgeting, your money is to divide it into three chunks as soon as you get it:

**1. Pay yourself first.**
Financial experts suggest setting aside 10 percent of all your income in a "rainy day," or emergency, account. The idea is to leave this money untouched, and regularly add to it, so you have cash on hand for unexpected needs. For example, if you hit a baseball through the neighbor's window and your mother says you have to pay to fix it, you might need a large amount of money at once. An emergency fund solves this problem.

## WHERE DOES IT ALL GO?

**Give It a Try, and DIY**

For one month, write down everything you spend money on. Everything. Include the obvious things (lunch with your friends, a new T-shirt, bus fare), but don't forget the little impulse buys—a two-dollar pack of gum, a 99-cent song on iTunes, or some lip gloss from the dollar store.

Make a chart, or **spreadsheet**, to track your purchases:

**Column 1 is the date you spent money.**

**Column 2 is what you spent money on.**

**Column 3 is how much you spent.**

At the end of the month, review your chart. Ask yourself these questions:

- **Where did your money go?**
- **Which categories do you spend most on?** Examples might include fast food, clothing, or games.
- **Do you have any money left over?**

What are some things you wish you hadn't spent money on? Where might you have saved money? Add up how much money you might have saved by making different choices.

## 2. Save to meet your goals.

The second chunk of money is the cash you've decided to stash to meet your medium- and long-term financial goals. Watch this grow until you're able to meet your goals!

## 3. Have some fun.

After the first two chunks of money are set aside, what's left is your spending money, your fun money, your day-to-day dollars.

Deciding how much money to save for your medium- and long-term goals, compared to how much you want to spend right away, can be tricky.

It's a bit of a balancing act. You might want to save *all*, or nearly all, your money, so you can buy that TV faster. But if you do that, you may not have enough money for fun—and that's not realistic. It's a sure-fire way to blow your budget. You'll get frustrated and just start spending.

If, however, you give yourself *too much* fun money, it will feel like *forever* before you get that TV.

Making these choices takes some thought. Ask the adults in your life to help you figure out this part of your budget. You'll be surprised at how quickly your rainy day (or broken window) account grows, and how exciting it can be to watch your TV fund grow. At the same time, you'll have cash in your pocket for fun—and for immediate needs. Most importantly, you are on the road to lifelong financial success!

**Weekly Income Budget**
(allowance, chores, baby sitting, etc.)
*$20*

medium- & long-term financial goals $13 • rainy day $2 • fun money $5

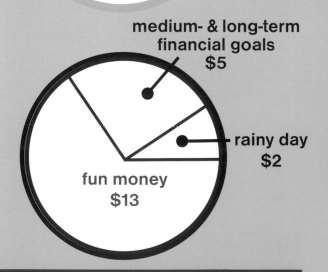

medium- & long-term financial goals $9 • rainy day $2 • fun money $9

medium- & long-term financial goals $5 • rainy day $2 • fun money $13

Here are three ways you might budget your weekly income. Which option seems to have the best balance between spending ("fun") money and saving for your financial goals?

| WHAT I WANT | WHAT KIND OF FINANCIAL GOAL IS THIS? (When will I be able to buy it?) | COST | WHEN I WANT TO BUY IT | HOW MUCH DO I NEED TO SAVE EACH MONTH? |
|---|---|---|---|---|
| movie & pizza with friends (once/month) | short-term | $12 | Now! | $12 |
| smart watch | medium-term | $60 | 3 months | $20 |
| smart TV | long-term | $280 | 8 months | $35 |
| bicycle | long-term | $540 | 12 months | $45 |
| video games magazine subscription | short-term | $36 | 2 months | $18 |
| designer jeans | medium-term | $100 | 3 months | $35 |

**NEED LIST May 1, 2017**

| WHAT I NEED | WHAT KIND OF FINANCIAL GOAL IS THIS? (When will I be able to buy it?) | COST | WHEN I WANT TO BUY IT | HOW MUCH DO I NEED TO SAVE EACH MONTH? |
|---|---|---|---|---|
| dog collar | short-term | $12 | Now! | $12 |
| birthday present for brother | medium-term | $60 | 3 months | $20 |
| concert tickets | long-term | $280 | 8 months | $35 |
| laptop | long-term | $540 | 12 months | $45 |
| cheap jeans | short-term | $36 | 2 months | $18 |
| art supplies | medium-term | $100 | 3 months | $35 |

# LET'S DO THE MATH

Give It a Try, and DIY

Time to fill in some columns in your "want" and "need" lists!

1. In the first empty column, write down how much each item on each list costs. In the second new column, write down when you hope to purchase each item.

2. Do the math to figure out how much money you'll have to save each month to reach your goal in the time allotted, and write that amount in the last column. To determine this amount, first divide up your income by each of the needs and wants. You may then choose to allocate more money per month to needs or wants that are most important to you.

3. Every time you reach one of your goals, you can start working on the next one!

# REALITY CHECKS

At this point in your life, the responsibilities of adulthood might seem a long way away. If they're so far into the future, why even think about them now? It's true that some aspects of adult life don't have to be on your radar just yet. When it comes to managing money, though, the best time to learn is now—*before* your life gets complicated with bills to pay, a house to run, or children of your own to raise. Besides, it might only be a few years before you need to save for college or your own car. If you work toward becoming a financial whiz today, your good habits and money smarts will last a lifetime.

**MONEY-WISE
FINANCIAL WIZARDS**

SAVE

Do you think you'll want to buy a home one day? For most of us, it will involve taking out a homeowner loan called a mortgage. Mortgages are usually paid off over a long time and at a certain rate of interest. So deciding to become a homeowner is a really big deal. In fact, it's probably the biggest single financial commitment most people make in their lives.

## Owe No Dough

One of the most important reasons to learn to manage your money now is to make sure you stay out of **debt** later.

Some debt is necessary. A person who wants to buy a house, for example, will probably have to borrow money from a bank or other financial institution. This debt is considered "good debt," because the borrower acquires a valuable **asset** (a house) with the money.

Other debt, though, is considered "bad debt," and it is one of the greatest causes of financial problems for people who don't budget. Simply put, people who spend more money than they earn often end up borrowing money to pay for things they can't afford to buy. This can eventually lead to a dangerous amount of debt.

## Interest is Interesting

Over time, the amount of money a borrower owes may increase because he or she also has to pay **interest** on it. Interest is the price a consumer pays for the privilege of using someone else's money.

Most interest is determined by a rate, or fixed amount. An **interest rate** determines how much money will be added to the initial **loan** every day, week, or month. The interest rate is usually measured as a percentage, or part, of the loan **balance**. (The balance is the amount owed on the loan.) For example, a 10 percent monthly interest rate means that 10 percent of the unpaid balance will be added to the total balance due the next month.

There are different kinds of interest on different kinds of loans.

## New Car Average Depreciation

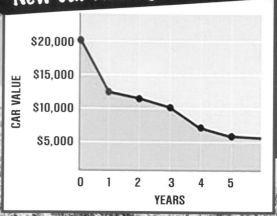

Because you can sell them, cars are considered an asset. But new cars, like the shiny red model shown here, also depreciate, or lose their value, in very little time. In fact, just driving a new car off the lot can reduce its value by 11 percent. This means that a new $20,000 car might be worth $2,200 less by the time you get it home! As this chart shows, new cars lose the greatest portion of their value in their first year. So it might make good financial sense to resist buying a brand-new car and instead look at cars that are slightly used, or new-ish!

# F⊙CUS ON FINANCE

## Assets and Liabilities

The money in your bank account isn't the only measure of your wealth. Many people have money tied up in assets—things they own that are worth money. An asset can be something big, such as a house, car, or diamond ring. It could also be something smaller, such as a baseball card collection, lightly worn clothing, or a nice piece of furniture.

Basically, anything you have that you could sell for money is an asset.

On the other hand, anything that takes money out of your pocket is called a **liability**. For example, loans and debts are liabilities.

Sometimes—just to confuse things—assets can also be liabilities. A car, for example, is an asset because the owner could sell it for money. On the other hand, it's a liability because an owner will never be able to sell the car for the same amount of money he or she paid for it. The owner will eventually lose money on it.

## Simple Interest

The most basic type of interest is called simple interest. This is the kind of interest you usually pay when you borrow money for a car or a house. At the time of your purchase, you agree with the lender on how much interest you will pay, and how long it will take to pay off the loan. If the interest rate is 10 percent, that amount is calculated as a percentage, or part, of the original loan. That percentage is then added to the amount you are borrowing, which is called the **principal**.

## Compound Interest

The other kind of interest that most of us experience is called compound interest. This is more complicated than simple interest, and it is the kind that most credit card companies use. Because you are likely to use credit cards even at this early stage of your life, it is especially important not to wind up spending more with a card than you can afford to pay back right away.

With most credit cards, interest is added to the unpaid balance every day, week, or month, depending on the loan agreement.

Simple Interest

Interest $200

Principal $2,000

**Total amount paid off over 1 year = $2,200**

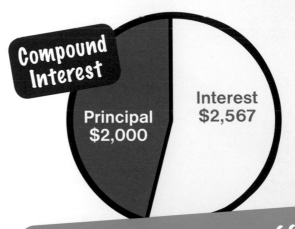

Compound Interest

Principal $2,000

Interest $2,567

**Total amount paid off over 8.5 years = $4,567**

This pie chart gives you an idea of how a car loan based on simple interest works. You borrow a certain amount of money at a certain interest rate, for a certain period of time. In this case, you are borrowing $2,000 at 10 percent interest. The time in which the loan will be paid off is one year. For a simple loan like this, the interest is simply added onto the original amount you borrow (known as the principal), and the combined principal and interest are repaid over the year in a series of 12 monthly payments of a little over $183 each.

This chart shows the same $2,000 purchase, but here you use a credit card with an interest rate of 23.1 percent. The payments are for both principal and interest. You have chosen to make only minimum payments of $45 per month. Each month's unpaid balance now includes compounded, or accumulated, interest on the balance from previous months. At this rate of payment, it will take you eight and a half years to pay off a balance that will grow to $4,567. That's more than twice the amount of the original principal!

## ASSESS YOUR ASSETS

Have you ever thought about how much things you own might be worth?

1. Make a list of things you own that might have value.

2. Search online or in stores, or talk to the adults in your life, to figure out how much you could earn if you sold these items. (For items that might be worth a lot of money, make sure your parents or caregivers know their value or what you've discovered online.)

3. Think about which items you would consider selling if you needed money in a hurry.

THINK FOR YOURSELF

### Go Figure!

Are you thinking of selling something to get some extra cash? Or maybe you'd like to trade something for something else. When figuring out the value of something you are thinking about getting rid of, consider sentimental and replacement value, not just the dollar value of the item. Think also about whether you'd even be able to replace the item in the future. If you need money in a hurry, which items would you be willing to part with?

For example, if you pay for an item with a credit card but do not pay back the entire amount at the end of the month, you are charged interest on the amount still unpaid. If you do not pay the full amount the *next* month, you are then charged interest on the whole unpaid balance—made up of the principal and any interest added to it. Month by month, debt is added to the money you owe for the items you have bought.

Before long, as the months go by, if you don't pay the entire balance you will continue being charged interest on the unpaid interest that has built up monthly. You are paying interest on interest! Also, if you pay late, or don't pay the minimum monthly payment, penalty fees may be added to your balance. These fees will be subject to interest, as well.

This is one way how, for many people who don't have financial plans and who borrow or spend money unwisely, debt can spiral out of control.

By making a budget, you'll know how much you can afford to pay for things. By following that budget, you'll manage to steer clear of this kind of dangerous debt, and ensure a healthy financial future.

## Lessons Learned

In this book, you've learned about financial planning, setting goals, and budgeting. That means you're already farther ahead in your financial literacy than many grown-ups are.

By setting aside an emergency fund, you've already begun preparing for unexpected glitches in life. If you continue this habit into adulthood, you'll always have money in the bank to deal with crises such as losing a job, your car breaking down, or a baseball crashing through your living room window.

You've already learned, too, that saving a few bucks out of your weekly allowance and birthday money means you'll eventually have cash for the bigger things you want in life.

As an adult, you'll make more money than you do now. Your long-term financial goals will also be bigger. Right now, your goal might be to buy a bicycle. In 10 years, your goal might be to purchase a car. By continuing your new saving **strategy** as you grow up, you'll know how to plan for that car—it will be a big reward for sticking to a budget.

Another thing you've learned is that it's important to plan for fun in your weekly or monthly budget. You don't need to **deprive** yourself of entertainment and social activities.

That might even become more important when the complications of adult life start to kick in. By then, though, you'll be really good at knowing how to balance your spending money with saving money. By then, you'll be a financially responsible, realistic, and savvy citizen.

# F⊙CUS ON FINANCE

## Smarter Than a Fifth Grader?

Recent studies show that American adults aren't the world's best at understanding money matters. As reported in a 2015 national financial literacy study:

*"Americans demonstrate relatively low levels of financial literacy and have difficulty applying financial decision-making skills to real-life situations."*

*The Wall Street Journal* wrote about a different 2015 study:

*"A sprawling global survey of financial literacy around the world finds that the U.S. ranks 14th, behind Singapore and the Czech Republic."*

The top nations in this study include Norway, Denmark, and Sweden (tied for the top three spots), Canada (tied with Israel for fourth/fifth place), and the UK (in sixth place).

These same studies show that most American adults do not have money set aside for emergencies, many cannot pay their monthly bills, and about one-fifth of them spend more money than they earn every year. Most adults surveyed said they wished they'd started learning about money—and saving money—earlier in their lives.

theft of credit card ID

stealing passwords

call me on this number

telephone fraud

email scams

pay now or you could be arrested

# BE CAREFUL OUT THERE

# DON'T BE SCAMMED!

Not everyone earns their money in honest ways. Greed leads some people to try to **scam** others out of their hard-earned cash. In recent years, many people have received telephone calls, texts, and emails from strangers demanding money. For example, scammers pretending to be from the government might send out a message saying, "You owe us money, and if you don't pay up, you're going to jail." Out of fear, many victims send money straight into the criminals' bank accounts.

Other scams involve trying to get people to give out personal and banking information by phone, email, or text message. **Legitimate** organizations do not operate this way.

Another way bad guys try to get other people's money is by leaving a message asking an individual to call a fake phone number. As soon as the **unsuspecting** person calls the number, it starts charging money to the victim's phone bill.

Remember to be suspicious about anyone asking you for money or personal information by phone, email, or text. If this happens to you, do not offer any information, and talk to a trusted adult right away.

# GLOSSARY

**asset** Something a person owns that is worth money

**ATM** Automated, or Automatic, Teller Machine; a machine that automatically provides cash and performs other financial services to an account holder who uses a credit card or debit card plus a personal security code to gain access to his or her account

**balance** The amount of money due on a bill or a loan; mathematically, the balance is the difference between the amount owed and an amount paid

**banknote** Paper, or folding, money, such as a dollar bill

**barter** To exchange goods or services for other goods or services without using money

**budget** (noun) An estimate of how much money comes in and goes out of a household or business in a given period of time; the amount of money needed or available for a purpose, such as running a household

**buyer's remorse** Regret for making a purchase

**circulate** (of money) To make coins or bills (by a government) as legal money and used as currency

**colony** A country or area under the control of a different country, often a distant one; a group of people who leave their homeland to settle in that new place; they are usually still connected to their homeland

**consumer** Someone who buys a product or pays for a service

**counterfeit** Fake

**cowrie** A specific type of seashell once used as money

**currency** Money used by a country

**debit card** A bank-issued card that allows the holder to withdraw money or pay for something directly from his or her bank account

**debt** Money owed to a person or an organization

**deprive** to deny a person or oneself things that are needed or considered important in life

**expense** The amount of money something costs

**financial institution** A business whose primary purpose is to deal with money; banks and credit unions are financial institutions

**glitch** A minor malfunction or setback

**holographic** Relating to an image that appears to be three-dimensional

**impulse buy** A purchase made without thinking, spur-of-the-moment

**income** Money earned or otherwise acquired

**inflation** A continual increase in the price of goods and services

**interest** A fee paid to borrow someone else's money

**interest rate** A portion of an amount owed, usually expressed as a percentage, that determines how much interest is added to the original amount

**invest** To purchase something now to make money in the future

**legitimate** Complying with or obeying laws and rules

**liability** Money owed, or something that will cost money for a person or organization

**loan** Something that is borrowed, especially money, that is expected to be paid back, usually with interest

**long-term goal** Something a person wants to do or buy in the future

**mad money** Money set aside for fun; spending money

**medium-term goal** Something a person wants to do or buy soon but not right away

**mint** To make coins

**mortgage** A loan to buy a home

**paycheck-to-paycheck** A situation in which a person or family meets all financial obligations with current earnings from one pay cycle to the next, needing all those earnings to survive until the following payday

**point-of-sale** The place where you pay for something—for example, a cashier's desk at a store

**polymer** A chemical compound made up of long strings of identical molecules; some are synthetic, such as plastic; others, including DNA, occur naturally

**principal** An amount of money that is invested or borrowed, and on which interest is due

**priority** Something that is treated as more important than other things

**receipt** A written statement that proves that certain money, goods, or services have been received

**savvy** Having practical knowledge, understanding, and ability in a particular area

**scam** To cheat, swindle, con, or rip off

**secure** Safe from danger

**shorn** Past tense of *shear*: to cut the wool from a sheep or other animal; used to describe the condition of an animal whose wool has been cut

**short-term goal** Something a person wants to do or buy very soon

**splurge** To spend money extravagantly: to indulge oneself in luxury

**spreadsheet** A computer document with columns and rows, often used for tracking incoming and outgoing money; the user can program mathematical formulas into a spreadsheet

**standardize** To conform to a fixed size, weight, quality, value, or other characteristic

**strategy** A plan for, or approach to, something

**taboo** Forbidden; prohibited or restricted by social custom

**tactile** Of or connected to the sense of touch

**transferable receipt** A receipt proving that precious metals have been deposited in a bank; the receipt can be used to purchase other goods and, at any point, the person in possession of the receipt can exchange it for the original deposit

**unsuspecting** Unaware of potential danger or harm; trusting

**virtual** Existing on, or by way of, a computer

**withdraw** To remove or take away

# FURTHER INFORMATION

## BOOKS

Chatzky, Jean. *Not Your Parents' Money Book: Making, Saving, and Spending Your Own Money*. New York: Simon & Shuster Books for Young Readers, 2010.

Dakers, Diane. *Money for Your Life: Invest in Your Financial Future* (Financial Literacy for Life). Crabtree Publishing, 2017.

Nourigat, Paul. *If Money Could Shout: The Brutal Truths for Teens*. FarBeyond Publishing, 2012.

Owen, Ruth. *I Can Have a Yard Sale!* (Kids Can Do It!). Windmill Books, 2017.

Thomas, Keltie. *The Kids Guide to Money Cent$*. Kids Can Press, 2004.

## WEBSITES

**www.themint.org/**
*The Mint* is a website designed to teach financial literacy skills to kids, teens, parents, and teachers. It includes information, games, and tools to help you learn. These three links are good places to start learning about planning and budgeting:

**www.themint.org/teens/saving-tricks.html**

**www.themint.org/teens/the-save-spend-plan.html**

**www.themint.org/kids/saving-tricks.html**

**www.usmint.gov/kids/index.html**
**www.mint.ca/store/content/htmlTemplate.jsp?cat=Kids%27+Corner&nId=1000008&node Group=Learn#.V_gGs5MrLo8**
These two sites—one U.S., one Canadian—tell you everything you need to know about how coins are made, the history of the U.S. Mint and the Royal Canadian Mint, and special coins in each country.

**http://read.marvel.com/#/labelbook/41238**
This link takes you to a free graphic novel, *Guardians of the Galaxy: Rocket's Powerful Plan*. In this book, Ant-Man, Hulk, Black Widow, and others join the Guardians in a money-saving adventure.

**www.pbskids.org/itsmylife/money/managing/index.html**
*Managing Money: Spending and Saving* is one of the life skills websites in the PBS *It's My Life* series. It includes advice, games, and tools to help increase your financial literacy.

# INDEX

## ABOUT THE AUTHOR

Diane Dakers was born and raised in Toronto, and now makes her home in Victoria, British Columbia. She has written 3 fiction and 18 nonfiction books for young people. Diane is a bit of a financial nerd. She enjoys budgeting, tracking her spending, and saving for future fun!